My George:

A Love Letter to My Dad

Life Lessons That Helped Mend My
Wounded Heart

I0418719

Kathy Butler

Dedicated to all the little girls and grown women walking around with a dad-size hole in their hearts.

And, to My George:

Your love has been woven into all my accomplishments, milestones, and triumphs.

But it has also carried me through my disappointments, losses, and dark days.

You are — and have always been — my dad.

Contents

My George:

Taylor

without remorse
to flourish

A Love Letter to My Dad

Foreword

"If you're going to ask God to order your steps, make sure that you're ready to move your feet."

Papa,

These are words that I will never forget.

In 2019, on the brink of making [arguably] the biggest decision of my life — YOU said these words to me. And while, at the moment, I was annoyed with what seemed to be your riddling choice of words and demeanor, those words later became illuminating instructions that have shed light on every big decision I have made since.

So, thank you. Thank you for these words. Because they have saved me from heartache. They have reminded me to stop and pray. They have reminded me that God's will is always better than

3

my own. And they were the start of a better life for me. Moving to Atlanta has truly made my life so much better, but I never would have done it had you not reminded me to move my feet.

Every time I yield to Christ's will for me and move further into my purpose — it's because years ago, I was reminded to move my feet.

Thank you!

~Taylor

Acknowledgments

Writing something so personal was hard because I wanted to be integral in telling these stories while being careful not to share more than those closest to me would be comfortable with the world knowing about us. With that in mind, I hope it is clear that I could not have done this without the support of my family.

To my mom: Thank you for loving me in spite of myself. I tested your patience in ways that no one will ever truly understand, but just as the Bible says, your love repeatedly covered my transgressions. You have always been there with open arms helping me to mend my broken heart and become the woman, wife, and mother I am today. You are truly the best mother for me.

To my husband: Thank you for encouraging me to push beyond my comfort zone and to believe in myself. You have always been my hype man, supporter, and my soft place to land. You gave me the space I needed to tell my truth without the fear of condemnation and shame. I love you. Till the wheels fall off…

To my children: Thank you for speaking life into my dreams when I couldn't always see my way. Your belief in me has given me the strength I needed to write this new chapter in my life, literally. You are 'my heartbeat' and 'my air,' and I am so proud to be your mom.

My George:

To
KATHERINE
WITH LOVE
4-11-10
GEORGE
Be Silent and Listen
To your Life . . .

A Love Letter to My Dad

Introduction

I remember being in the tenth grade standing on the quad of my high school. I was having this conversation with another girl. I don't even remember her face or her name now. I just remember the conversation because it was the very first time I opened up to someone about my "daddy issues." I was telling her how I didn't understand why my biological father didn't want me; didn't fight for me and left me like it was nothing. I was crying and just needed answers. Because the way I saw things at the time, if my own father — the one man who was supposed to love me first and forever — didn't want me, that had to mean there was something wrong with me. It was reminiscent of that scene in the Fresh Prince of Bel-Air where Will breaks down in Uncle Phil's arms and asks, "How come he don't want me, man?" I actually tear up every time I see that scene because I feel every bit of it – every time.

Of course, I didn't get my answers that day on the quad, but I eventually got to interrogate my biological father. Sadly, that discussion left me with even more wounds, but it also set me straight on one thing. My dad — the man whom I affectionately call "George," and who raised me as his own since I was a toddler — was there all along. I just hadn't seen the beauty in what God had done for me by giving me exactly what I needed before I ever realized it was missing.

The truth is, my biological father may have abandoned me for reasons I won't go into at this very moment because he died many years ago and it is what it is. But right now, today, I can look at George — my dad — and without any hesitation, I can say, "It was you!" It was you who fathered me, filled, and covered that man-size hole in my heart like a perfectly cut graph installed by the hands of the most skilled surgeon.

This collection of stories is my love letter to you — My George — to show you just how much I appreciate all the ways in which you've shown me the true love of a dad. And, how grateful I am for the real-life lessons you've taught me from the beginning. Because, as far back as I can remember, it was YOU who was there all along.

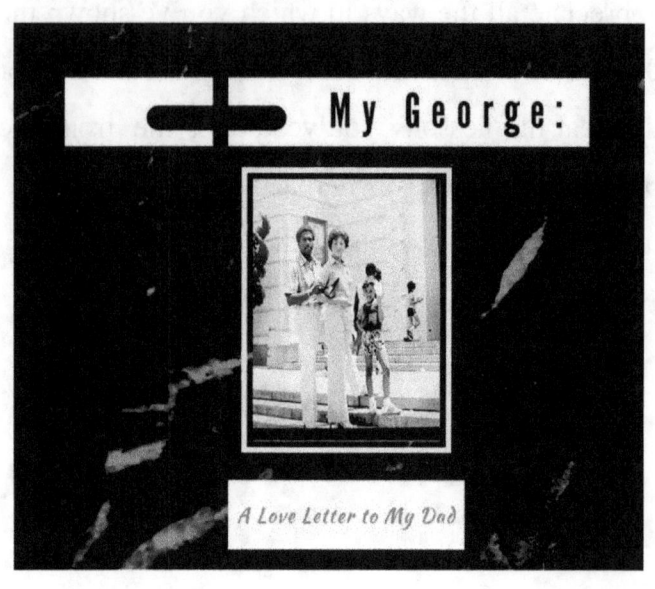

My George:

A Love Letter to My Dad

The World Just Might Pinch Back

Many people talk about the terrible twos when referring to their feisty, head-strong, and sometimes even bratty toddler. Well, I was all of those. I was the youngest granddaughter on both sides at the time. I was also the youngest sibling. So, imagine the havoc I was allowed to wreak. In fact, as a teen, my grandmother constantly reminded me of the things I had said and done to the dismay of the adults around me. To this day, my older cousins will remind me about how much I got away with and how they couldn't understand why the very things they got popped for were cute to the adults when I did it.

However, in my defense, I spent days on end with my grandmother, her siblings, and friends, so I was exposed to A LOT. Not in an abusive way, but in an "I heard all the gossip and knew all the grown folks' business" kind of way. That made me, well sometimes, hell on wheels if you know what I mean. I can recall snatching my grandmother's boyfriend's cane away from him one evening because I didn't want him to leave. When he took it back and began to walk away, I screamed, "Well, go ahead and leave you ol' cripple!" That hurt his feelings and I of course was made to apologize, but you get my point. I could be a real terror sometimes.

Well, it was My George who showed me that everybody wasn't going to stand for my shenanigans no matter how cute the world told me I was. He was talking to my mom about something — I don't even remember what, which is fine because that's not the point. The point is my mom was standing right there. Anyways, as they were talking,

I got in the middle of the two of them because I wasn't quite getting the attention that I wanted. I proceeded to pinch the fleshy part on the top of his hand so hard that I drew blood with my little razor-sharp nails. He said ouch and quickly pulled his hand up to assess the damage. After asking me why I did it and me explaining that he wasn't giving me the attention I wanted at the time, he did the unthinkable. He pinched me back! And I mean hard. I started to cry from the sheer pain, but I was also devastated because I couldn't believe he would do that to me. Me, the cute kid that everybody adored and let get away with murder.

In the moments after, he explained to me and my mother, who was also pissed about it, that sometimes you get back what you give out. That would be the equivalent of today's colloquialism, "matching energy." For the Christians, it would simply be reaping what you've sown. And for those who are for the streets, "if you want some a**, you betta bring some with you." Needless to say, my mom didn't appreciate the on-the-spot life lesson that he had just doled out, but it definitely set me straight. He quickly let me know that he didn't care how cute I was, he was not about to let me intentionally hurt him without a swift response. He also told me and my mother that if I didn't get that nasty behavior under control, one day someone else could potentially do far worse to me than just pinch me back. He didn't say this in a hateful, you're a terrible person kind of way. But more so in a tough love, "I don't want someone to truly harm you one day because of your own stupidity," kind of way.

I tell this story from time to time and people sometimes remark that they can't believe a grown man would do that to a little girl. Or they question what type of man would do that. But, for me, it was one of the most loving things anyone has ever done for me. He showed me how the real world really works and that actions have consequences. Especially, for a Black girl in America. The world is harsh and doesn't care how loved and adored I am by my tribe. If I set out to cause harm, it may just come back on me. So, I must always be intentional about moving in a way that does right by others and to others.

This was written inside one of the many inspirational journals that My George randomly sends from time to time.

Respect Is Just the Minimum

So often we hear that Black women are the most disrespected and unprotected people in America. Many of the women I know have stories on top of stories detailing all the ways in which they've been disrespected and experienced fear when engaging with the opposite sex. Sometimes the disrespect is hurled from bigoted strangers who fail to see our humanity, while in other instances, it can be the petulant behavior of a bruised ego when a guy's attempt at getting our attention fails. Or it can be someone we know who simply doesn't value us the way they should. Whatever the case may be, it is unacceptable, and I learned that at an early age.

I was about nine or ten years old and we lived in an apartment complex on a fairly busy street. All of the units were situated above the parking garages, which meant there was no street-level view of the sidewalk from any of the apartment doors or windows. It would have been very easy for a passing car to snatch a kid up and keep going before anyone ever noticed. This is why I always skated around the courtyard of the building instead of on the sidewalk. My George was also the manager of the building we lived in and the one next door, so I knew most of the residents and of course, they knew me.

On this particular day, I skated from our back porch and around the bushes that sat in the middle of the courtyard. As I rounded the last stretch, I passed by the window of a longtime tenant whom My George often had words with because they didn't pay their rent on time (remember, I was always around when grown folks were talking). But, since the tenant was related to the buildings' owner, there wasn't much that he could do about it. This tenant also seemed to always have a live-in boyfriend and sometimes the boyfriend would take on the same attitude expressed by the tenant towards My George, which was the case this time around.

I guess the boyfriend found the sound of my skates moving across the concrete to be quite an irritant even though it was the middle of the day when one would expect kids to be outside playing (back when kids stilled played outside). He came flying out of the apartment and began barking at me about making too much noise, and how I was disturbing his nap even though he didn't work. This was just another tidbit I learned from grown folks talking. He began demanding that I go play somewhere else, but I wasn't trying to hear that. So, I said something smart like, "You can't tell me what to do," and I kept skating. He then said something semi-threatening to me that ended with "And tell yo' daddy I said that!" I eventually went in the house and didn't mention the encounter to my older sister who was home with me at the time. But I knew he had no business talking to any child like that, especially me, because My George had made it clear he didn't tolerate disrespect. Nor, did he play about his family.

When my parents got home that evening, they were preparing to go to some black-tie event, so they were both scurrying around getting all gussied up. My George finished getting dressed before my mom and emerged from their room wearing a dapper black tuxedo — owned, not rented — with all of the accessories, including cuff links, a very nice watch, and his signature gold link bracelet. He also smelled amazing per usual; his hair was freshly cut and lined up, and his hands were thoroughly moisturized. He looked like he was ready to grace the cover of GQ magazine.

I came around the corner from the kitchen and met him right outside their door. I began to explain how I was playing in the courtyard earlier that day and the dude across the way came out and told me I was making too much noise. I told him what he had said to me in a semi-threatening tone and ended with, "And he said tell yo' daddy I said that!" My George yelled out, "He said what?" along with a few other choice words that I won't repeat. Before I knew it, he grabbed his blackjack — a piece of steel that's covered in leather and fits perfectly in your hand — which was conveniently in reach, and he was headed out the backdoor before my mom could catch him. She asked me what was going on so I told her what the guy had said, and she looked at me as to say, "Why would you tell him that right now knowing we have somewhere to go?"

She took off after him and I after her, but we were too late. We could already hear the sound of him banging on the apartment door where the live-in boyfriend resided while screaming the name of the actual tenant. The boyfriend opened the door not realizing he had poked the bear by talking crazy to me and then seemingly daring me to tell My George what he had said. By the time mommy and I turned the corner, the boyfriend was up against the wall outside of the apartment with his shirt balled up in My George's hands right underneath his chin. Expletives were flowing out of My George's mouth and the blackjack was positioned right in his face and ready to do damage. The guy was apologizing profusely and tried to reassure My George that he didn't mean anything by it; he clearly wasn't thinking straight, and he was just tired when he said it. He was also insisting that it wouldn't happen again. All the while, the tenant was pleading with him, "Mr. G, he didn't mean anything by it. Please let him go."

Eventually, he heard my mom calling his name and emerged from the rage he was in. He let the guy down, but not before giving dude a few more choice words that let him know he wasn't *ish*, his momma wasn't *ish*, and well, you get the drift. He then began adjusting the jacket of his tux and continued to reiterate that the boyfriend should refrain from saying anything else to me or the next time, he was going to go to put that blackjack to use, and neither my mom nor the actual tenant would be able to save him. The boyfriend was visibly shaken and when he lifted his head, I was smirking right at him from behind My George as to say, "Yep, I told my daddy."

Now for the record, I don't tell this story to advocate for violence, although it is necessary sometimes, but rather to illustrate that it was My George who taught me that respect from a man — all men — is just the minimum. It also reminds me that I should always feel protected by the man in my life because My George, my first protector, always made me feel safe. I knew without a shadow of a doubt that My George would go to war for me, even in a designer tux, if necessary. And any man in my life better be willing to do the same.

My George:

A Love Letter to My Dad

A Man Keeps His Promises

Bright lights! Slot machines! Showgirls! Yes, I am talking about Vegas baby! Sin City! The Vegas of old when the Sahara hotel was jumping and before there was a Bellagio. The Vegas of yesteryear where you still had to pull the arm of the slot machine. The Vegas that gave me chills as I heard Natalie Cole belt out "I'm catching hell," and although I didn't truly understand what she was singing about, I felt it. The adult playground where fortunes are won and lost. The town where anything you can imagine is available, both legal and illegal. The home for coveted residencies for entertainers and their look-alikes. And, the place where I spent an inordinate amount of time as a child! Why? Because although my parents had five kids between them, I was the youngest and all of my siblings were grown and out of the house. We had no family that lived nearby and my parents didn't have "close friends" whom they trusted like that. So, quite frankly, they simply didn't have anyone to leave me with.

My George liked to gamble, so he was invited to tournaments regularly. And if there was one thing he never turned down, it was an invitation to Sin City. That four-hour drive was like a walk around the block for him. We would hit the 10 freeway and we were at the McDonalds in Barstow before I knew it. You know, the one that is made from old train cars. My parents would order me a happy meal; make me go to the bathroom, and then we were back on the road again. Within a few hours, we were making that descent into the bright lights and onto the Vegas strip.

I remember being in the back seat of the car as we drove toward the Las Vegas Hilton excitedly anticipating whose face would grace the marquis. At that time, it was a coveted venue for any entertainer to play. It was also the place where I was introduced to and developed an appreciation for, so many different art forms. As we entered the brightly lit driveway and approached the valet, the excitement of the city was palpable, and even as a kid, I wondered what new thrill was in store for me each time. A new show I hadn't seen; winning another big stuffed animal at Circus Circus, or maybe meeting a new celebrity and taking a picture that I could send to my grandfather.

Usually, we checked in, dropped our bags in our room, and within minutes we were headed down the elevator. My parents would walk me through the casino, past all the gaming tables, slot machines, and shops until we arrived at the arcade. They would give me a $10 roll of quarters and a speech — "Don't leave this arcade! Don't talk to strangers. If anyone bothers you, tell security and come and get us."

Typically, I would run out of quarters, defy my parents' instructions, and begin to meander through the beautifully appointed hallways of the hotel taking note of the colors and patterns in the carpet and the ornate pieces of art on the wall. I was convinced that the inspiration for the décor was taken right from the corridors of a palace because it seemed so regal. Hues of gold, burgundy, and navy. Ceilings that captured masterpieces of baby angels floating on clouds, none of whom looked like me, but that's a discussion for another day. I would stop by the windows of the shops to admire the exquisite gowns, sparkling diamonds, and all of the high-end fashion accessories on display. The sight of it all made my eyes dance because I am a true girly girl at heart. Not to mention, I am also the true namesake of my great aunt who loved a sparkly frock, stiletto pump, and a red lip. But I digress. Eventually, I would make my way back to the casino where I would walk the perimeter of the floor until I spotted one of my parents.

On this one night, I found my parents sitting at the slots and My George seemed to be doing fairly well. I told them I had run out of quarters and needed some more to keep playing games in the arcade. He dug into his bucket and gave me a couple of handfuls. He told me to give him some luck, so I kissed his cheek. Then, I asked for the Gucci purse I had just seen in one of the shops as I made my way from the arcade. He smiled at me and promised to buy it for me if he won. And back off to the arcade I went.

Before the weekend came to an end, he hit big, and I reminded him about his promise. He pulled out a few chips, cashed them in and we proceeded down the beautifully appointed hallway until we reached the shops. We walked in and just like that, I had my first Gucci purse. But even better, that purse became a simple, yet powerful symbol of what it looked like to have a man fulfill his promise. This demonstration of integrity became woven into my psyche and created an expectation that a man says what he means and does what he says he's going to do. It became the blueprint and standard that I measure every man against to this day. It's also one of the many qualities that my girls love most about their dad, because I was blessed to marry someone who not only takes pride in being a man of his word, but he has also taught his girls to require nothing less of a man.

My George:

A Love Letter to My Dad

I Got You!

Let me begin this essay by saying that this wasn't one of My George's finer moments, but it is what it is. He was the captain of the 'You Gon Learn Today' squad before Kevin Hart made it a household saying. Back then, there were no cell phones capturing every moment for social media likes and clicks, which is the bedrock of what we know today as cancel culture. Because if it were, My George would have definitely gone viral for this one, and The Shade Room debate about whether to cancel him or declare his innocence would have no doubt garnered him his fifteen minutes of internet fame.

Picture this. It's the 80s. We are in the main showroom of the Las Vegas Hilton (yep, another

Vegas story). The room was packed. You could hear the roar of the crowd that reverberated with chatter and laughter. Hostesses walked about taking cocktail orders and returning with libations galore. Glasses clinked as people toasted to winning big; getting hitched, celebrating another year around the sun, and any other occasion you can imagine. The lights were dim as we awaited the main act to hit the stage. The only problem was the billows of smoke that were choking me and my mom coming from what seemed like an eternal flame of the cigarette being held up by the lady sitting right in front of us (well, kinda below us). Not only was she holding it so the smoke flowed in our direction, but with every drag she turned her head and blew the smoke over her shoulder and right towards us! I coughed and fanned, but there was no escaping it.

Now keep in mind this was way before smoking in public spaces was outlawed. These were the days when it was completely normal to see people driving around with all the windows up; a cigarette hanging from their mouth, and their kid(s) in the car. So, after a few comments to My George and him seeing how miserable the smoke was making my mom and me, he leaned forward and politely asked the woman who appeared to be late fifty-ish, maybe sixty-ish to reposition her cancer stick away from us and send her dragon-like clouds of exhaled smoke in a different direction. She barely acknowledged him with what appeared to be a look of entitled annoyance as she returned to her conversation with the folks sitting at her table. And the billows continued.

The main act finally took the stage and everyone seemed to be having a marvelous time. Everyone except us that is. We were still being strangled by the fire-breathing dragon lady in front of us and My George was growing more and more annoyed with her with each cough and subsequent gesture we made to clear the air. I watched him look at her, almost through her, with annoyance. It was like he was trying to will her into developing an ounce of common courtesy and human decency at that moment. But alas, it wasn't working. I watched intently as he sat his drink down and every so often, he pushed it further and further towards the edge of the table. This went on for what seemed like an eternity, but in reality, it was probably all of ten minutes.

Once the drink was right at the edge of the table, he looked subtly around the room and then looked at my mom to seemingly apologize in advance for what he was about to do. Then, he did it. His fingertips gently pushed the glass right off the table and the waterfall landed right down the back of the fire-breathing dragon lady. Her back arched as she gasped from feeling the ice and liquid falling down the back of her cream silk blouse. Immediately my mother shot My George the most disapproving look and his eyes seemed to say, "I said sorry in advance."

As the woman turned around and scowled, My George turned on the charm. He said, "Oh dear, I am so sorry about that. It just slipped right off the table." He was appropriately contrite so as not to appear as if he had purposely just stained and likely ruined what looked like a very expensive blouse. He even offered napkins to her and her companions to dry her off, but she was inconsolable and stormed off.

I smiled at him and chuckled deliriously on the inside. He shot a coy smile back at me and we began to enjoy the show sans the smoke. That night I was so mesmerized by how he was so calculating in how he effortlessly slew the fire-breathing dragon lady. Even more so, I realized once again that he simply didn't play about me. His look said, "even if it seems like I can't fix it, just wait. I got you!"

My George:

A Love Letter to My Dad

There Is Enough of You to Go Around

If you know My George, you know he isn't one for "traditional" church. I mean, he went. But he definitely has his own way of looking at religion. So, it was a real adjustment when my mom expected him to attend church every Sunday. And although he reluctantly obliged, he needed something to anchor him. That something became his leadership role with the Young People's Department.

I remember spending Friday evenings and Saturday afternoons at the church while my parents worked with the youth. It was a real thrill for me because I was younger than them and I thought it was so cool to be able to be around all the older kids. In fact, my friends often commented about how unfair it was that I got to be at all of the teen events when they weren't allowed because they were too young. To make matters worse, many of the teens were the older siblings of my friends, and the fact that their siblings were nice to me irritated them even more. But my parents had no one to leave me with, so again, I was in tow wherever they went.

My George was a tell-it-like-it-is, tough love type of youth leader. He gave the youth room to be youth while the other youth leaders had seemingly unrealistic expectations for them. He knew they were still figuring life out and that they were bound to make bad decisions, use inappropriate language, and be a bit girl/boy crazy. He also gave amazing pep talks and even gave a hug every now and then to young men who were raised to believe men don't cry and weren't often shown affection. This made the young people gravitate to him even more.

There were two young men in particular who seemed to be drawn to him. Mike was the desire of many of the girls and he knew it; while Mel was rough around the edges and although he wanted the girls, they didn't always want him. They were close friends so when you saw one, you always saw the other and most people often viewed them as one big pain in the butt, except for My George. He saw them as two individuals who just needed guidance and someone to show them that they were worthy of love.

He spent countless Fridays, Saturdays, retreats, and summer programs mentoring them in his own way. Some days they accepted it and some days they rejected it, but he kept pouring into them regardless. There were a couple of occasions when one or the other stormed out in anger because the rap sessions triggered some uncomfortable emotions, but that didn't faze him. He would walk right out behind them and talk to them man to man. Those conversations were private so I can't tell you exactly what was said. But, I could definitely tell he made an impact because their stance would slowly shift and they would soften right before him.

Once Mike and Mel graduated from high school, they stopped coming to church and My George lost contact with them. He was saddened to learn they both lost their lives to senseless violence a few years later. But in the end, he knew he had done everything he could to show them the "dad kinda love" they so desperately longed for. In doing so, he ultimately showed me that there was enough of him to go around. As a result, I could freely share him with other kids without ever feeling like I wasn't a priority or being envious of the attention any of them may have received. I guess this is also why I admire this same trait in my husband, because much like My George, he goes out of his way to make sure each kid he engages with feels seen, heard, and important.

My George:

JUST A THOUGHT

I HAVE MADE MISTAKS
I CANNOT CHANGE,
BUT I HAVE MADE CHANGES
TO NOT MAKE THE SAME MISTAKES.

DAD 2021

A Love Letter to My Dad

Just Don't Lie to Me

Throughout my childhood, I had a level of freedom that some Black kids couldn't relate to. I was able to speak my mind freely in our home and outside of our home as long as I wasn't outright disrespectful. My mother says that was a huge parenting blunder on their part because I was a little too free at times, and she was always getting calls or being pulled to the side about something I had said. She would usually hold her head in shame and feel the need to apologize (LOL). However, My George was far less moved because he thought people too often said things they had no business saying in the first place, and they often said it to children as a way of making kids feel inferior. Or, because they knew most kids were taught to "respect their elders" even if the elder was as he would say, "full of (expletive)." But I digress, again (LOL).

Some would wrongly interpret this level of freedom for a Black child as a lack of structure or home training, but it was far from that. It actually required a lot of communication that was built on one cardinal rule in our home — DON'T LIE TO ME. And although there were only a couple of occasions that I got caught in a lie, they were life lessons I never forgot. One in particular, happened when I was about 11 years old.

My parents were big on reading for pleasure as a way to increase my vocabulary and writing skills, as well as to keep my mind sharp during downtimes like spring and summer break. From the time I was enrolled in school, I always had workbooks that I had to complete outside of school. Eventually, we had regular visits to the library and I had to do book reports for my parents. Yes, I said my parents — not school! So, on this one particular occasion, My

George had picked up this book for me and I was tasked with reading it while he was away on a trip. I guess it didn't occur to me that he was going to ask me about it because it wasn't a book that I had chosen at the library, which were the ones that I typically did book reports on.

He returned from his trip about a week later and we are having this casual conversation while he is unpacking his things. I am sitting at the foot of the bed and just asking him about the trip and he is asking me what I had learned that week. You know, just basic chit-chat. Then the conversation turned to the book. Now keep in mind I thought I was slick, so I had read a few pages of the beginning and a few pages of the end. Enough to give me the gist of the storyline, or so I thought. It also never occurred to me that he had read the book! And there were some important life lessons that I would soon discover he wanted me to take away from the book. As he asked me questions and I gave these ambiguous and generalized responses, he began to realize I hadn't actually read the book.

At that point, he turned to me and asked, "Did you read the book?" I, with bold-faced confidence, lied straight to his face and said I had. He asked me a few more questions that one could only know the answer to if they had read the book, and again my answer was vague and wrong. He asked me again, but this time looking me dead in my eyes, "Did you read the book?" With dropped head and countenance, I said "no." The look on his face was one that I did not soon forget. He was HURT. Not angry, but hurt. Then, with tears in his eyes, he simply said, "Why would you lie to me? I thought we were better than that?"

Those words still haunt me as I write this essay because at that moment, I had broken something that meant everything to him — his trust. It was the thing that our love and bond had been built upon. He trusted me and I definitely trusted him. I trusted him with everything because he was there for me by choice. He wanted me and all he asked for in return was honesty. And just like that, I thought I had ruined US forever. But true to fashion, he asked me why I lied. We played the "I don't know" game for a minute, but he didn't relent until I gave him my truth. "I was afraid I was going to get into trouble," I said.

He gave me a long lecture about the value of being trustworthy and how your reputation is all you have. He told me that violating trust can take years to repair and for us in particular, it was such an unnecessary breach of our relationship because after all, what was the worst that could've happened if I had just fessed up to not reading the darn book? A lecture? Being placed on punishment? It wasn't like I was going to be hit or harmed, so why would I rather risk being characterized as a liar instead of just telling the truth? We were better than that, he said, and he knew that he had proven himself to be someone who could be trusted with my truth. With tears in his eyes, he reminded me that he loved me and nothing would ever change that. He also said he would be there for me through anything, all he asked was "just don't lie to me." And with that, we hugged and wiped our tears and I learned to recognize what the essence of love felt like.

My George:

A Love Letter to My Dad

My George

My memories of you go back so far, I can barely remember when you weren't there.

Even though I know you weren't. I also know that you didn't just choose my mom, you CHOSE me and my sister too. And in doing so, you didn't come in with demands about titles as a way of solidifying your place in our lives. Instead, you rested comfortably in your role because you knew exactly who and what you would become to us. So, when I think back to all the times someone questioned why I call you George and not dad or daddy, I am reminded that "George" *IS* how we say dad in our family. You are — and have always been — MY dad. Sadly, everyone didn't understand our dynamic, but they learned (LOL).

I was about 12 years old, and we were at church one Sunday morning. I probably had on my favorite gray suit, satin blouse (even though I wanted silk), and kitten heels that you and mommy bought me because I always wanted to look just like her. And you were too happy to oblige. Service had ended a few minutes prior and everyone was walking around the courtyard greeting one another and making small talk as we did most Sundays after church. I had lost sight of you and I was probably looking for you to ask for money to buy something like cookies or a piece of cake.

I saw Mrs. H, a prominent leader in the church, and asked, "Have you seen George?" She replied, "I don't understand why you call him by his first name. I think it is so disrespectful for kids to call their parents by their first name!" I immediately responded with, "Because that's his name and that's our business." Of course, she had a look of shock and horror on her face because that too was disrespectful as far as she was concerned, but I didn't care. I walked off in search of you again, but this time I was on a different mission.

When I finally found you, I immediately told you what Mrs. H said to me and I even fessed up to what I said to her in response. My mom was flustered and trying to tell me that I can't always say what comes to my mind when talking to adults, but you looked up and began to scan the crowd and took off in her direction. Mommy was on your heels trying to get you to think before you spoke, but as usual, when it came to your family, that battle was lost before it even began. You belted out her name as you approached her so there was no mistaking that you were coming for her, and the look on her face said she knew she had said something she had no business saying.

You began to question her about what she said to me and she tried to justify her comments by explaining that she thought it was disrespectful for kids to call their parents by their first name. You looked at her and basically said, "Why in the *Sam Hill* is it any of your business what my child calls me? You have crossed the line." You gave her a few more choice words, and quite frankly, none of it went over well considering we were STILL ON CHURCH GROUNDS! But true to form, you couldn't care less. When all was said and done, you made sure she apologized for overstepping and making me feel some kind of way about our family dynamic.

At that moment, I was soooo proud that you were My George. You let me and everyone else within earshot know in no uncertain terms that there was absolutely nothing wrong with our family dynamic and how we loved. I knew that while I wasn't "born" your child as a result of a moment of intimacy between you and my mom, I was conceived in your heart. You hadn't simply chosen to marry my mom, but you also chose to be my dad. And you didn't care if I called you George, dad, daddy, father, pops, or any other colloquialism one could offer, you would fiercely protect our bond against anyone, anywhere. This is also the reason it tickles my soul every time I hear my kids call you Brown Sugar — even in public. Because that's simply just another way for them to say Papa and that suits you just fine.

My George:

A Love Letter to My Dad

The Talk

One of my favorite podcasters, Demetria L. Lucas, writes these delightful "Dear Mum" posts to chronicle her #seesomeworld travels. She originally started writing the posts as a way of helping to keep her mom's nerves under control because they let her mom know she was alive and well, especially when she was traveling internationally. But they quickly became a way for the rest of us to see the world through her vivid descriptions and illustrations of her day-to-day travel activities. Reading them always makes me a little sentimental because they bring to mind all the trips we took as a family when I was a kid. My George has always been adamant that Black children should not be deprived of seeing the world beyond our own neighborhoods. He also says traveling is just one of the ways that Black children learn to dream.

We mostly took road trips, so I've seen much of the U.S. from the back seat of our big brown Mercedes sedan (yep, I'm an old-school Sheila E. fan). We would generally load up the car and head east, although we spent a lot of time up and down the California coast as well. One of our most memorable trips was to Washington D.C. where we saw all the national monuments, including the White House. We took so many pictures one day only to discover when we got back on the road that evening there was no film in the camera. We laughed about that for years! We also went to The Alamo, Albuquerque, the Grand Canyon, New Orleans, Seattle, The World's Fair, and Canada. But the trip that shaped me the most and changed me forever was in the summer of 1984.

We were taking my sister to college in Louisiana. We had been traveling for what seemed like forever, but, it had probably only been like a day and a half. My sister, stepsister, and I were growing restless and hungry, so we pulled off the freeway in a small town in Texas. I can't even tell you the name of the town because, at that age, I wasn't accustomed to paying attention to that kind of stuff. I just looked for the signs with food and gas logos. However, I do remember having this eerie feeling about the place as we exited the interstate and made our way down the main thoroughfare of this small town.

It was almost as if things began to happen in slow motion. The people on the sidewalks; in the businesses, and in other cars began to stare at us like we were exhibits at the zoo. Mouths fell open as people turned and pointed in what seemed like anger, but that made no sense because they didn't know us. As we entered the parking lot of the local diner, my mom, sister, stepsister, and I all insisted that we weren't *that* hungry and commented that we should get back on the interstate. But My George was unfazed and refused to be intimidated by the stares, and although we were basically pleading with him to leave, he told us we were going to have a good meal and instructed us to get out of the car.

When we entered the diner, we were, of course, the center of everyone's attention. And I mean, everyone. We were seated and I can't even recall what I ordered. I just remember feeling wildly uncomfortable and wanting to get out of there as quickly as possible. When the food arrived, my mom noticed there was a hair in her eggs. She brought it to the waitress' attention who made light of it and suggested that she should just pull it out. My mom was rightfully pissed off, so My George demanded that the waitress take the plate back and have the cook remake my mom's food. Ultimately, the waitress complied but my mom was certain that they had just pulled the hair out of the original plate, so she refused to eat. Me, my sister, and stepsister scarfed down our food as quickly as we could so we could hurry up and get the heck outta there, but My

George ate at his usual pace refusing to allow anyone to disturb his meal.

We noticed people had begun to gather outside while we were eating, but once we exited the building, we saw the crowd had grown substantially. As we made our way to the car, I was scared and didn't truly understand what was happening. My mom, sister, and stepsister were afraid as well, but My George calmly told us to get in the car. As we pulled out of the parking lot and turned onto the street, people began shouting at us to leave their town. If that wasn't bad enough, as we approached the fire station, the firemen turned their hoses on full blast in our direction basically flooding the streets within seconds causing our car to hydroplane. Then, it went from bad to worse.

Out of nowhere, a pickup truck with confederate flags, reminiscent of something I had seen on the Dukes of Hazard, came flying around to the front of our car at top speed. There were several guys in the cab and several more in the back. And they were mad! They were shouting, "You niggers get out of our town!" They had cans and bottles in their hands and were waving them in a threatening gesture as to say they were going to throw them at our windshield. By now we are all panicking; everyone except My George. He told us to calm down, stop all our screaming, and just sit back. All the while, he never took his eyes off the truck as it swerved back and forth in front of us.

He slowly leaned forward, eyes still locked on the truck, and he reached under the seat. From under his seat, he pulls out a Crown Royal bag and my mom shrieks in disbelief, "You brought your gun?" With his eyes still trained on the guys in the truck, he slowly rolled down the window, stuck out his left arm with the bag in hand, and placed it decidedly on top of the car. Then he looked one of the guys dead in his eyes and said, "Try it (expletive)!" The guy must have read his lips because immediately, he yelled to the driver that My George had a gun and they needed to abort the mission.

They sped off and My George drove calmly to the interstate with the gun still on top of the car. Once we safely turned onto the interstate, he put the gun back under his seat. And in a most irritated tone, he reminded us that he has always got us and there was no need for us to panic and scream the way we had (insert eye roll from all of us…LOL).

As we made our way down the interstate, he gave us "the talk" *again*. The one all Black parents must have with their kids periodically to help protect them. He lectured us on how racism is alive and well, and how we always needed to be prepared because racist people will try us. And how you have to let them know that if it's you or them, then it's gonna be YOU! Needless to say, I remained in shock for a few hours. I had literally seen the face of evil that day for the very first time and it appeared in the expressions of men, women, and even children who didn't know me or my family. We were complete strangers to them, but they were willing and ready to harm us simply because we were Black and as they angrily chanted, "didn't belong" in their town.

If I am honest, that day changed me forever. It shaped me as a person and forced me to view the world and white people through the lens of that day. Even now, I sometimes wonder if a white person that may be standing behind me at the grocery store, sitting beside me at work, or singing in the pew behind me would have behaved like the men and women of that small town if they were there that day. Sadly, the fact that I am not always sure is the scariest part of it all, even after all these years.

However, at the insistence of My George, I have seen some of the world — domestically and internationally. I've been wowed by the splendor of clear water, pink sunsets, white sand, and majestic mountaintops. And yeah, it made me dream bigger and reach for greater. But sometimes it reminds me that there is an evil that lurks simply because I am a Black girl and I draw breath, so as My George always says, I keep my head on a swivel.

My George:

A Love Letter to My Dad

Actions Have Consequences, But My Love Is Unconditional

I was 14 years old when I went on a church retreat (remember the word 'church', because this one is a doozy). I was so excited to go because some of the best times of my life were spent with my church friends. Many of us grew up together, so our bond was extremely tight, and we never missed an opportunity to hang out together — summer camp, vacation bible school, Saturday afternoon rap sessions, youth day field trips — you name it, we were there. This event was in February. I remember, because to my surprise, my mom had snuck a few new outfits, some Mrs. Fields cookies, and a Valentine's Day card in my bag so when I opened it everyone was oohing and aahing about it. SN - My mom has always been great about giving THE most thoughtful gifts and making us feel special. But, back to this retreat.

On this particular retreat, my BFF who had not been around as long as the rest of the crew came along as well. He had only been hanging out with us for a couple of years, compared to some of the rest of the crew who had known one another since they were toddlers. I had met most of them when I was about 8, so we still had a considerable amount of history. Some of the crew weren't huge fans of my BFF because he had a bit of a rebellious streak and was no stranger to trouble, but I looked passed that because deep down he was really a nice guy and a blast to be around. On this particular trip, he assured me we were going to have fun and he would make sure that if trouble found us, I wouldn't have to take the heat for it.

Fast forward to the following evening, he pulls out a bottle of gin (yes, at the church retreat!). He usually chose gin as his drink of choice because it was supposed to be odorless and could be easily mixed with some type of juice to make it less distasteful. When my other friends got wind of alcohol being present, they warned me against it, but I didn't have the good sense to listen. The party girl spirit had already jumped on me and I was down for a good time even if it meant pissing off some of my crew. So, the shenanigans started, and I can't even tell you how many drinks I'd had before some of my friends realized I was pretty twisted and began trying to talk me into going back to the lodging area to sleep it off.

Eventually, after much prodding and probably a few threats, I acquiesced and went back to the lodging area. But I didn't actually go to sleep. Instead, we sat around, talked, and I began snacking on Doritos and other junk food that didn't mix well with the gin or the juice. And although my friends were trying to hide the fact that I was wasted from our chaperones, some of whom were parents of my friends, the truth was getting ready to come out — literally.

About an hour or so later, my stomach began to turn and I ran straight towards the bathroom with a friend or two behind me. I was hurling into a toilet in sheer embarrassment to a chorus of 'I told you so' echoing behind me. They were still trying to hide me from the chaperones until my friend's mom pushed her way into the bathroom and there was no denying the stench of alcohol-scented vomit hitting her nostrils. She was sooooo disappointed in me because she watched me grow up and she knew I knew better, especially at a church retreat! She dismissed my friends, got me cleaned up, and gave me a stern but compassionate talking to about peer pressure and how there was plenty of time to "party" when I was of age. My parents were called, and I was forced to return home for breaking the rules of the retreat.

Needless to say, it was a long ride home because I just knew my parents were going to kill me for the obvious embarrassment the situation was going to cause them. After all, we went to one of the premier bourgeoisie Black churches in the city at that time, and all the parents wanted everyone else to think they had it all together, including their kids. Of course, the kids knew it was all pomp and pretense because kids talk, so we were well aware of what was really going on behind those bougie facades.

Sitting at that kitchen table and seeing the look of disappointment on my parents' faces was just as painful as if they would have just picked up a belt and handled things "the old-fashioned way," but My George was never one for physical punishment. His words were his rod of correction. So, I had to sit and listen to a lecture before my sentence was doled out to me. Somehow, I ended up in the basement with My George having yet *another* conversation that started with "Why did you do it?" It wasn't a question that I was really prepared to answer because at the end of the day, did it really matter, and did I really even know? So, I said what most teens say when being pressed for a response to a question they aren't fully prepared to answer, "I don't know."

That was not good enough for him though. He just continued to press. He then asked did I know why he and my mom were so disappointed and that was a question I could definitely answer. "Because I embarrassed you," I said. And to that he responded, "I couldn't give a rat's a** about what those people think, you know me better than that!" He went on to say that I was his only priority and my thoughts about myself and the decisions that I made were what most concerned him. That said, we were back to "Why did you do it? What did you get out of it?" I finally broke down and simply said I just wanted to have fun and fit in. "Nowwww, we're getting somewhere," he said.

That took us down the road of what seemed to be a two-hour conversation about peer pressure, the danger of fitting in, and the ultimate cost of leadership. Yes, I said the cost of leadership. Because as he explained, "It's easy to go along. Heck, it can be quite comfortable. But going against the grain and being willing to stand alone, that's going to cost you. It may even cost you some "friends" and it won't actually feel good, but you'll have to decide if you have what it takes to stand alone." He then thanked me for being open and honest, rebuked me for thinking I could ever be an embarrassment, and reminded me that actions have consequences. But love — his LOVE — was unconditional. And there was nothing that would make him stop loving me, not liking me at times, absolutely (LOL), but not loving me…never.

Those words guided me through so many rough days and bad decisions. Those words have anchored me when I wanted to end it all because I know that type of love comes from a place deep within. It is not fleeting, superficial, or easily moved. It is rooted and inextricably tied to the soul of the person who possesses it and to lose the person to whom it is tethered, means you inevitably lose a piece of yourself. And you'll be left with a void that simply can't be filled. Knowing this, I've had to fight through some dark times to keep from creating that void in My George's heart.

My George:

A bend
in the road
is not the end
of the road,
unless you fail
to make the turn.

A Love Letter to My Dad

Inspirational clipping from My George
Quote attributed to Helen Keller

Boys Want One Thing, But It's Your Choice

G rowing up, most of my girlfriends would've told you that the idea of talking to their dad about boys was never even a consideration. After all, both moms and dads typically shared a similar refrain about keeping your dress down, panties up, and your nose in the books. But not My George. He was extremely practical and not delusional in his understanding of basic human sexuality. He understood that as we matured into our teens, we were going to become more interested in boys and yes, even sex. So, he didn't shy away from the tough questions.

I can recall conversations in the car about liking boys and what was permissible (i.e., kissing, groping, intercourse) and what wasn't. He wasn't one to rattle off talking points about abstinence and purity, but instead, he talked about making decisions that would serve me well. He made it clear that having desires was normal, but what you did with those feelings could change the trajectory of your life. He was also adamant that yes, boys will definitely try to move you towards having sex. That's what's on their minds! But that didn't mean that I had to do it. It was always my choice.

Because of this, I felt a bit of freedom in understanding that I could decide if I wanted to engage in any type of intimacy; who I wanted to engage in it with, and where. I didn't need to feel as if I owed myself to anyone and my NO definitely meant NO. That's also the reason why I had no problem fighting a few guys off as a teen. I shouldn't have had to because they should've understood the principle of consent as well. But, someone clearly failed to reinforce that lesson for them, so my knee and nails did!

We also had conversations about dating someone who wasn't Black and there again, he laid out the facts. He explained that it wasn't up to him to dictate who I chose to date or even marry. However, he didn't want me to be disillusioned about the world we live in. Interracial dating and marriage have their own set of challenges and regardless of whether it's unfair, unjust, or flat-out wrong, we must be clear about the realities of this life and go into situations eyes wide open as opposed to eyes wide shut. Now don't get me wrong, he IS as pro-Black as the day is long, but he has never been the type to beat his chest about anything. He is going to give it to you straight and I do mean straight. Then, he will stand back and let you make your own decisions.

Because of this, I was free...in ways that many teens couldn't relate to because all they knew was condemnation, judgment, and fear. Now that's not to say that I always made good decisions, I just knew I had to live with them. But I also ALWAYS had a quarter taped to an index card in my wallet courtesy of My George, because bad decision be darned, I could ALWAYS call, and he WAS coming.

My George:

A Love Letter to My Dad

I'll Love You While You Find Your Way

This essay just might be the hardest to write because I need everyone to understand that my mom and My George didn't deserve what I put them through, and my immaturity caused a level of pain that was not easily remedied. It also forced them to make the hardest decision in their lives concerning me. But they never gave up on me. And while you may feel like you would have done things differently, life has taught me that it's easy to judge other people's decisions until it's your turn.

At the age of 15, my feelings of abandonment by my bio dad sent me into a spiral of sorts. I had long struggled with not understanding how the person who participated in my conception had just walked away without so much as an explanation. I mean, he literally just stopped showing up years prior for the court-ordered weekend visits that he fought for when I was about 9 years old. Granted, I do recall that I started telling him I had other things to do because I grew frustrated with the normal routine of him picking me up on Friday evenings; immediately dropping me off at my grandmother's house, and then coming back for me at 5:30 pm on Sunday evening to ensure I was returned home by the court ordered 6:00 pm drop-off. I wanted to spend time with him, but he had other priorities. I really struggled to understand how he could walk away so easily.

We had moved to a new house the summer before seventh grade, so I convinced myself that after the move he didn't know where I was, and that's why I hadn't seen him for years. There was even a night when things exploded at home and I yelled out in anger to My George that he wasn't my real dad. As awful as it sounded coming out of my mouth for the first and only time, and as hurt as he looked, he simply responded with, "Well I'm the one that's here and I love you." But that didn't seem to eliminate this need to connect with this illusive being who I made out to be a martyr of sorts in my own mind to avoid having to face the facts. If I was as important to him as I thought I should have been, he would have moved heaven and earth to find me and be my dad.

Inevitably, I began acting out in ways that are usually attributed to girls with "daddy issues." Unbeknownst to my parents, I was drinking regularly and became promiscuous. Most people would have characterized my behavior as that of a spoiled, bratty teen because I lived in a nice home in what was considered a nice neighborhood. I had two parents, designer clothes that my mom would just bring home after spending her lunch hour in the mall, and we went on vacations pretty regularly.

Yet, I couldn't shake this need to know why this man, my biological father, found it so easy to leave me. I needed to know why I wasn't enough. And then something happened that created an opportunity for my questions to be answered.

One afternoon out of the blue, I was at school and someone approached me and said my brother was looking for me. Confused, I asked if they were sure it was me they were looking for because while I knew I had a brother, I hadn't seen him in years. As far as I knew, he, nor anyone on my biological father's side of the family knew where I was. He eventually found me and when I say he was excited to see me, that would be an understatement. He told me how he had gone to different schools around the city over time looking for me. We talked for a bit and he assured me that the rest of the family missed me too.

Not too long after, I convinced a friend of mine to take me to my grandmother's house whom I hadn't seen since my father stopped coming around. I hadn't been there in at least 6 years and honestly only knew my way by using landmarks from memories of repeatedly traveling the same route every time when I was younger. So, one afternoon after school, we made our way to the route and found my grandmother's house. She was beyond happy to see me.

We got in the house and she immediately called my father and said, "You'll never guess who is here." Fifteen minutes later the man whose presence had eluded me the better part of my life was standing in front of me with a smile as wide as the ocean and his eyes were dancing with joy. He told me he thought about me every day and how much he loved me, which was confusing because years had passed, and he hadn't come to find me. But I needed to believe him. I needed to feel like I mattered to him, so I ate it up.

He gave me his phone number and I snuck off to see him and my grandmother a few more times over the course of the next month. We also talked regularly over summer break while I stayed with my other grandparents down south. He told me that he wanted me to live with him and how living with him would be so much better than living with my parents, because I wouldn't have all the "rules" at his house that my parents had (in retrospect, they were *normal* rules). Like a foolish young girl with daddy issues, I believed him. I began running away from home and acting out in ways that made my parent's life miserable, and eventually, they decided to allow me to go live with him not too long after my 16th birthday.

This was the most agonizing decision they ever had to make concerning me. My George was heartbroken, but he didn't try and stop me. After leaving home, it took a while before I went back to visit my parents. When I finally did, it was awkward. I was returning to the place and the people who had nurtured me my entire life, but I wasn't sure what to expect. But My George always showed me the same tender love and grew solemn when it was time for me to leave. It was like he was losing me again and again, and that had to be some kind of agony.

As the years went on and I had my own children, I realized what it cost My George to watch his whole heart in human form walk out that door into the arms of a man who didn't possess the depth of character to love me the way he had since I was small enough to stand on his feet as he danced me around the living room. He would have willingly exchanged his life for mine at any given moment without hesitation, if necessary, and I ignorantly walked away from that because of what quickly became the empty promises of a man whose own demons and addiction ruled his priorities. My George knew this man was incapable of nurturing me with the same level of care and devotion that he offered, but he also loved me too much to force me to stay. He knew I had to learn the ugly truth for myself and he loved me deeply enough to let me find my way. Of course, that path led me right back to him time and time again. Be it for advice, a hug, or to simply sit in the same room while he silently listened to his music because I just needed to be in the presence of someone who loved me unconditionally and thought I was enough.

In fact, years later after my relationship with my bio father was strained yet once again, I got the call that he was dying and wasn't expected to live more than a few days. I grappled with whether I should go and see him because in many ways I just didn't feel as if I owed him that. But after much counsel from my pastor, my husband, friends, and even my mother, I acquiesced to the urging. When I arrived a few days later, he lay in the home he had made for his "new family," eyes set and unable to speak. I stood there basically furious because I realized that once again, I had been asked to put his needs ahead of mine. He got to be in my presence one last time, but without being able to even mutter the words of the apology I felt he owed to me for abandoning me time and time again. An apology he had told me several years prior I wasn't going to get because he made no apologies for how he chose to live his life.

In those final moments with him, I told him how My George had been there to pick up the pieces of the heart he left shattered. How My George was there for all of the important moments, so I never had to be the girl who didn't have "a father" in attendance. How My George was a better man because he chose me from the beginning and never left even though I had given him reason to. How at the end of the day, I thanked God that his mercy and grace gave me My George and I wasn't subjected to the inevitable trauma that growing up around him would have inflicted. Then, I shocked myself and thanked him for having the decency to step aside and let the better man do what he knew he was incapable of doing. He couldn't speak so the tears flowed down his face and with that, it was me who turned and walked away.

That was the last time I saw him. Because the next morning when I arrived at the house, I got to the top of the landing in front of the door, turned around in what felt like slow motion, and realized the black suburban that was pulling away from the curb was actually the coroner carrying his body away. There were no tears for me at that moment because it didn't feel like my dad died. *My dad* was My George. This was merely the man who made my life possible, but chose not to actively participate in it. Eventually, weeks later, the tears came. But they were tears of "what might have been" had he only had the capacity to see me and love me like My George.

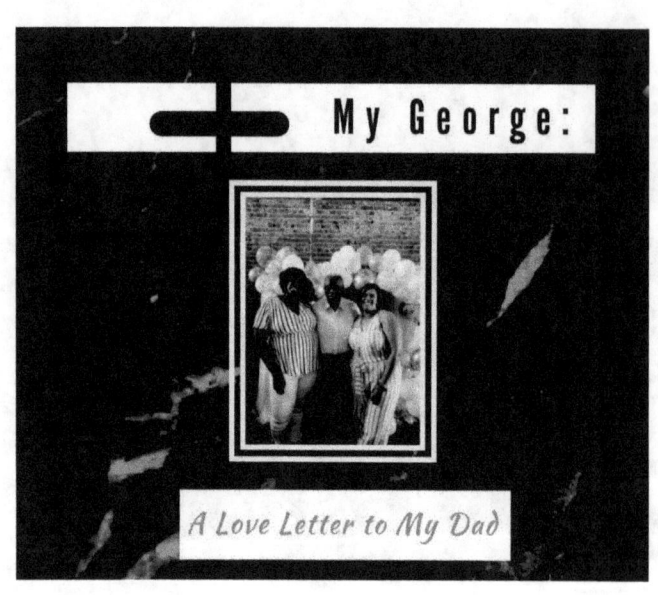

My George:

A Love Letter to My Dad

Brown Sugar

Watching My George with my girls has been one of my life's greatest joys. I think raising five girls gave him a pretty good head start because he was already well acquainted with the tears, the moods, and the know-it-all attitudes that can come with the day-to-day experiences of being a "girl dad." I mean, he had seen it all — boy drama, hair styles gone wrong, fashion mishaps, girl fights, and academic challenges. So, when my girls were born, he was ready!

He was never the sappy kind of grandfather who bowed to the wants and whims of their cute little grandchild. He wasn't moved by tears or tantrums. He refused to communicate using babytalk and by the time they were ten or eleven years old, he was having full on intellectual conversations with them about world events, culture and their future. And when they got into trouble, they received the same extended lectures that I got as a kid, including the inquiries about why they did what they did and what they got out of it.

He has always treated them like their opinion mattered and albeit he may have used the ol' 'because I said so' line a time or two, that definitely was not his standard refrain if they questioned him about anything he said or asked them to do. He has always given them the exact same space to speak their mind, ask questions and state their objections during conversations just as he did with me. And to my dismay, he even encouraged them to do the same with me. His rationale was always, "Well I encouraged YOU to have a voice and you turned out alright, didn't you?" And of course, I couldn't argue with that (LOL).

Somewhere around the time my youngest was in middle school, he began to refer to her as his Brown Sugar. It was such an endearing term that spoke to his love for her and her beautiful brown skin. Almost immediately, she began to call him that too. Then, the term took on a life of its own. My girls were calling him Brown Sugar, my mom was calling him Brown Sugar, I was calling him Brown Sugar, and even my friends were calling him Brown Sugar. He loved it!

I remember one occasion when we were at my daughter's school for an awards ceremony right before her high school graduation. All of the kids were yelling out "Hey Brown Sugar" because over the years he had attended Grandparents' Day and other school events and they had heard him calling her that and vice versa. She was somewhat embarrassed because after all, everything involving your parents and grandparents is embarrassing at that age. But she quickly moved passed it and it became a running joke between her and her friends from high school to this day. Whenever they reconnect, her friends will jokingly refer to her as Brown Sugar; immediately ask how *her* Brown Sugar is doing, and recount a memory about something he said or did during a visit to the school.

My oldest has her stories about how he has entertained her friends as well. There have also been plenty of days when she showed up at my parent's house looking for advice or comfort and in My George's own special way, he would listen; ask her to solution for the problem, offer his extremely *colorful* commentary, and then leave her to make the best decision for herself. Rarely is he ever going to flat-out tell someone what to do. He'll offer his opinion, but ultimately, you'll have to discover the best road to travel on your own.

As the years go by, I see My George's imprint on my girls in so many ways. Yes, they are indeed their father's daughters, but their Brown Sugar is definitely in there too. Be it my youngest daughter's unfiltered wicked sense of humor and unbridled tongue, or my oldest daughter's direct way of communicating. He has given them the same steadfast and unconditional love and wisdom that he has consistently given to me. He constantly reminds them that they are — in the words of Donna Hathaway — young, gifted and Black. And that is something to own, be proud of, and never forget nor diminish for anyone.

The healing aspect of seeing my girls with My George has been the fact that they have never known a time when their grandfather was not there. He has been a constant in their lives. They don't even know my biological father, nor were they subjected to any of the trauma his presence would have inevitably brought. They bare no scars or any unfulfilled expectation. For them, Brown Sugar is and always been their Papa. He has been ever present and I'm so grateful they've experienced his love.

My George:

K.B.

If you ask God to order your steps... be ready to move your feet.

Luv Ya Dad/George

A Love Letter to My Dad

Easy Like Sunday Morning

Sometimes when I am riding down the street with the windows down and the music playing, I am transported in my mind to the backseat of our family car where I learned one of life's most valuable lessons from My George — slow down and take it all in. I always found it odd that we lived about 12 minutes from our church, but it literally took 25 minutes for us to get there on Sunday mornings. Not because there was traffic. Not because we had to make a stop. Simply because My George drove at what seemed like a snail's pace. Slower than usual for sure.

This pace was also accompanied by the melodic sounds of 94.7 The Wave radio station. Oh how I hated that station most of the time. It was boring! I wanted to hear something upbeat like R&B or hip hop. Heck, I would've settled for just about anything else as long as I didn't have to hear what I referred to as the sleepy music. It felt like torture being in the backseat while My George drove at a snail's pace listening to music that pretty much lulled me back to sleep.

One Sunday, I was just over it so I asked My George why he insisted on listening to the sleepy music on the way to church, and why he always drove so slow on Sunday mornings? His response was simple, "I'm not in a hurry and I like to take it all in." To which I was like, "Huh??" He went on to explain that even though we took the same route every Sunday, he rather enjoyed taking in the community — the sounds, the scenery, the people. He said we didn't always need to be in a hurry. Sometimes we simply needed to slow down and appreciate the things and the people around us. And Sunday mornings was his time to do just that. He took note of the people and businesses that had served the community for generations. He took a moment to appreciate the murals that lined the boulevard symbolizing our pride in our culture. And of course, the scent of Leo's BBQ and Johnny's Pastrami being carried on the wind, which were culinary delights within the community.

Years later I found myself often taking the slow scenic route just like My George. Be it on the way home from work or out for a leisurely drive along the coast with my family. My hubby and I would turn on the melodic sounds of that same jazz station and take it all in. We especially enjoyed this time together to block out the noise of our otherwise hectic life and enjoy the serenity of the waves and gentle breeze. And when our kids complained about the boring music and asked why we couldn't listen to something else, I would simply tell them to sit back and enjoy the ride because we are taking it easy like Sunday morning.

My George:

A Love Letter to My Dad

Father of the Bride

I can't speak for all little girls, but I know there are many who spent their childhood dressing up their dolls and performing fake wedding ceremonies. They imagined their wedding day — their dress, the cake, their bridesmaids, the bouquets. And, the groom! Would it be a perfect spring day in a packed church filled with fresh flowers? Or maybe a warm summer day on the beach where a perfect breeze would catch her veil in the wind? Would it be a winter wonderland affair replete with all the regalia of Cinderella's ball? The possibilities were endless.

My wedding? It was an intimate affair on a Saturday afternoon in a soul-saving station. We had a handful of attendees; modest décor, and I wore a beautiful white, pearl-embellished dress. But I was missing a very key component, the father of the bride. That's because I didn't tell my parents I was getting married until the very last minute — as in, the night before. I knew they wouldn't approve because much like many other parents, they would have preferred I went to college, found a career path, and then considered marriage and a family. However, I wanted something different and instead of talking to them about it in a mature fashion, I fell back on old habits. Just like the evening I left home at 16 years old, I didn't thoroughly weigh the consequences or the impact of my actions on them at that moment either. It had become one of my life's greatest regrets. But God!

Fast forward years later, my husband and I were celebrating our 20-year wedding anniversary. He, along with our kids and our dearest friends, planned the fantasy wedding we couldn't afford the first time around. I was told I was going to be taking family pictures that day, so an appointment was made for me to get my hair and make-up done. I was escorted to the venue by my GFF, and when we arrived, I had all types of questions (iykyk!). We pulled up at a building along the Long Beach coast literally right on the beach. I made my way into the building with my family photo ensemble in tow and entered a dressing area where I was expecting to change for the photoshoot. My goddaughter pops out from behind a curtain separating us from another room, and in her hand was a beautiful box made of seashells. Inside was a beautiful silver sparkled veil and a note that read:

> We've known each other by CHANCE,
> became friends by CHOICE,
> still friends by DECISION.
>
> And, when we say FRIENDS FOREVER,
> that's definitely a
> Lifetime Promise!
> SURPRISE!!!!

Today WE celebrate 20 years together
with family and friends.
I LOVE YOU!

Then, out pops my husband and my girls with a beautiful strapless, silver, bedazzled gown that was fitted to my daughter, so it would require minimal alterations. But not to worry because her godmother, a phenomenal seamstress, was also on hand to make the on-the-spot alterations. My mom came in a little while later and helped me with some of the final touches, which was a moment in and of itself. Because although we had mended our relationship many years prior, not having her at my wedding still weighed heavily on me, so this moment felt like redemption. But that wasn't all....

When the doors opened and I saw My George was standing in the hallway to walk me down the aisle, my heart melted like ice cream on a summer day. His face lit up with pure joy and I could feel the shackles of extreme regret release me immediately.

We both had tears in our eyes as we stood there together, just he and I. He told me that he loved me and that he wouldn't have missed this moment for the world. He also made some corny joke and we both laughed. Then, he — My George, MY DAD — proceeded to walk me, his "lil frog," down the aisle just like a father should.

This was indeed the greatest gift we could have given to one another. He deserved to walk by my side for this moment and I needed him there. He had earned the title 'Father of the bride' YEARS prior, and I felt so immensely proud walking arm in arm with 'My Dad' through the warm sand almost to the shoreline where my groom awaited, again. He truly received his flowers that day and if that weren't enough, everybody on the beach got to see him looking just as fine as frog hair...HEYYYYYY BABY!! (Again, iykyk!)

My George:

When you get to be
my age, you don't
sweat the small stuff...

~G.W.G.~

A Love Letter to My Dad

One of my favorite songs is

"In Case You Don't Live Forever"

It tells the story of a kid telling his dad how much he loves him —*just in case*.

Its lyrics were truly my heart's song and desire as I penned some of my most cherished memories of you.

I pray each word finds a home in your heart just as I have.